LANDLORD KING

David Callahan

With Keith N. Haley

ISBN 13-978-1500-4785-20
ISBN 10-1500-478-520

LANDLORD KING

David Callahan

With Keith N. Haley

TABLE OF CONTENTS

CHAPTERS

CHAPTER 1

INTRODUCTION TO THE WORLD OF THE LANDLORD

What can be more important than home? We were born and raised there. Home is where we build our most loving and lasting relationships. Home is both our physical and emotional shelter. Ask a military veteran, especially one that has endured combat, what it means to come home. It means just about everything to the vet.

Home is where we grow and mature and also retreat to when we need solace, help, and love. As it has been said, "Home is where the heart it."

Who creates this home? The structure of the home (a house, an apartment, a duplex, or a condominium) is provided by a building contractor. That profession is not an easy one. Parents, of course, acquire houses or other structures for the members of the family by means of a purchase or a rental lease. Adults, of course, without children need a home of their own too and they do that by rental lease or purchase. Either option for acquiring a place to live is a major decision in a person's life. Cost, community safety, structural appearance, and internal furnishings are all critical factors in deciding where to live.

The Landlord and Common Law

A very large percentage of Americans rent or lease their residence, i.e. the home, they live in. The person who provides the lease is often referred to as the landlord, a term going back to early England.   The landlord owns the property, sets the terms for the lease or rental agreement, and creates the rules to be followed that will provide for a comfortable and civilized habitation. Supported by the common law, the landlords can set stringent rules that, in effect, make them the equivalent of a "ruler" or "king" in the minds of some. The process has worked in providing homes for residents for centuries. Lest we forget, the landlord owns the property and is responsible for the home's upkeep and the care of its immediate surroundings. That requires attention and diligence on the part of the landlord, for sure. Just think of some of the tenants that we have all known or known about who do little or nothing to keep a property clean and safe.

Occasionally the regulations and other burdens on landlords are more than excessive. St. Paul, Minnesota once tried to make landlords responsible for the amount of crimes in the neighborhoods where they owned and leased properties. Landlords and community activists resisted that overreach by government and won.

The Responsibilities, Burdens, Joys, and Sorrows in the Life of a Landlord

What are the responsibilities, burdens, joys, and sorrows in the life of a landlord? Let us say from the start that it is an "all day and all night" job. It is not a job for everybody.

This book will take you on a journey with a most successful landlord, David Callahan. Starting at age 7, painting walls for 25 cents an hour, David Callahan has spent 52 years in the property ownership, management, and maintenance business. As a landlord he oversaw 54 properties with approximately 500 tenants over the more than five decades of his career. One of his tenants was in a Callahan residence for 35 years and departed when he was more than 90 years old. David must have known him well and obviously the man was an excellent tenant.

This book will take you on a journey with one of the nation's most successful and entertaining landlords. He has experienced about all you can encounter in the role of the landlord, one many, if not most of us, could not perform in at all. David's stories and experiences will open up to you the details of a landlord who got involved with the business as a child working with his family that owned, leased, and managed properties in Columbus, Ohio. Truly after you read his book, you will agree that David Callahan is the "Landlord King."

This book will cover the major features of a landlord's life and responsibilities interspersed with a variety of stories taking you through a variety of emotions commonly experienced by a landlord. The eviction experience is only one of the many interesting, trying, and emotional activities a landlord engages in. You will see that what some tenants do is almost beyond belief.

Below are some of the major content features of the book, all including some landlord/tenant episodes that will be very enjoyable reading:

* The world of the landlord – major responsibilities, problems, and issues

* One man's story of how he became a landlord

* Properties and the kinds of lands "to rule"

* The nature and types of tenants

* How to select the "right tenant"

* Oh, my! The wrong tenants

* Major tenant problems and solutions

* It's time to leave – the problems and perils of eviction

* Allies in the "good fight" - bailiffs, judges, law enforcement officers, property manages and "good luck"

* The best landlord/tenant stories

* Conclusions and tips for those new to the landlord role

CHAPTER 2

HOW I BECAME A LANDLORD KING

Inching into the World of the Landlord

I imagine that few people grow up thinking about becoming a landlord unless it is bred into them from a parent or relative. That was my case. I was 7 years when I started painting walls for $.25 an hour at rental properties and by the time I was 17 years old I was repairing faucets, painting exteriors of homes, and doing other various and sundry tasks related to maintaining homes and apartments in the best condition possible. These properties belonged to my father or a close friend of his that he worked with at Kroger in Columbus, Ohio. My father devoted 34 years of service to the Kroger corporation.

My dad's colleague from Kroger became a landlord and his son was a friend of mine. I did some labor work for them also before my father got into the landlord business. I worked at Kroger also and was at the same store for about 5 years. I was responsible for keeping the dairy carts clean and filled. That was a job with little down time, for sure.

But I did other jobs also. I spent time working as a golf caddy at the Columbus airport golf course. At the age of 16 I became a cook at the state fair for the Bob Evans restaurant company. Doing that on a regular basis made me a little tired of sausage as you might imagine. Obviously I was no stranger to work as a child or a young man.

By age 18, I more than suspected that the course was set for me to be involved in the business of real estate. By age 35 I was a permanent fulltime employee on my dad's payroll. There was no bargaining involved in arriving at my salary. He alone determined my salary. But that was not all that I did in those early years. I worked my way into the business of being an expert provider of windows, doors, and insulation resulting in my own enterprise from 1994 on known as *Windows by Callahan*. What had I not down relative to property outfitting and maintenance by that period of time in my life? But the "worst" and "best" was yet to come. I was well on my way to becoming a landlord king, a position that few people could do at all, let alone do it well.

My father had worked so hard and passed on the same inclination concerning work to me. He was a career meat cutter for Kroger. At age 40, he remodeled his own home. How many would try that? Few would, indeed. He also bought two brick double-homes and paid $8,500 for each one. He also bought a property in 1972 for $12,000. In 2011, dad sold that property for $325,000. One of the rentals he had went for $60 a month in 1955. When he sold that rental property years later, the property rented for $600 a month! Yes, he was indeed good at the selection of rewarding investments. He taught me a lot about that.

At age 82, my father stopped driving and handed me the keys to his vehicle and passed on the authority to be our family's landlord king. He did not use those exact words in the transfer of power to me but that is what you are when you own, manage, and maintain 54 properties.

My dad reached 85 and by that time I was in charge of all the properties and yes, I was the landlord king. I thought I knew everything about the "kingdom" and its growth and maintenance, but there was so much more to learn and experience. The rest of this book will take you deep into the world of the landlord king.

If you have your mind and heart set on being a landlord, the pages that follow will be very helpful in preparing you for what you may encounter. For the rest of the readers, the book will be eye opening, full of surprises about the world of the landlord, and may even create a little sympathy in your heart for those who take on the role of the landlord since the job is not easy and requires determination and tenacity that few of us have.

CHAPTER 3

THE PROPERTIES AND LANDS TO RULE

If you have the capital to invest in a rental property of some kind, the difficult decision has to be made as to the type of property. With years of experience on the "landlord king throne" that choice is a lot easier, but many do not start out that way unless all of the investment property is handed down from parents, other relatives, etc., i.e. previous "rulers." I was very fortunate indeed being able to sit at the right hand of my father as he took the initial steps to invest in a property and built his landlord kingdom and passed on his wisdom to me. Those property investment decisions are complex in nature and have major consequences as one might imagine. Some are rewarding and others can be devastating.

What Are the Properties a Landlord King Can Own?

Look out your window in any direction and you will get some idea of what a landlord king can own. Vacant land, apartments, condominiums, single person and multiple person dwellings, business and office property, a parking lot, a junk yard, a trash and recycling piece of acreage, campsites, storage facilities, hotels, tourist homes, farm residences with land, etc. A landlord king could even lease land for a prison, jail, halfway house, or school but these are properties that my father and I never considered. There must be special issues associated with those acquisitions. We rented dwellings to the best tenants we could find and as you will see later in the book choosing and interacting with tenants is not all joy, for sure.

The Landlord Obligations under Law

Every state has its own set of legal requirements that the landlord must follow, but, of course, there are similarities. Chapter 5321 Section 04 of the Ohio Revised Code lists the obligations that landlords must follow. A brief summary of those obligations is below:

1. Comply with all of the following codes: building, housing, health, and safety;

2. Make all repairs to keep the premises in a safe, sanitary, and habitable condition;

3. Maintain in good and safe working order and condition all electrical, plumbing, sanitary, heating, ventilating and air conditioning fixtures and appliances, and elevators supplied or required to be supplied by the landlord;

4. When the rental agreement covers four or more dwelling units, the landlord must provide appropriate receptacles for the removal of ashes, garbage, rubbish, and other waste incidental to the occupancy of a dwelling unit and arrange for their removal.

5. Supply running water, reasonable amounts of hot water, and reasonable heat at all times unless the building that includes the dwelling unit does not require it by law or unless the building is so constructed that the heat or hot water comes from an installation which is within the exclusive control and supplied by a direct public utility connection.

6. Except in the case of an emergency (or if it is impractical to do so) give the tenant reasonable notice of the landlord's intent to enter and enter only at reasonable times. Twenty-four hours is considered to be a reasonable amount of time for that notice if there is no evidence to the contrary.

There are indeed other obligations for landlords and tenants to follow, but these are the essential requirements the landlord must live by. Other matters will be addressed in my stories and incidents of dealing with tenants in later sections of the book. For the moment just imagine all of the issues and problems that can arise over implementing and abiding by the landlord's obligations. In addition, some tenants want far more than what is required of even the best and most attentive landlords. As you will read later, some of those issues and problems will be surprising and near beyond belief.

The Tenant Obligations Under the Law

Tenants have to live up to the law in Ohio also. Can you imagine that some do not from almost day one of the occupancy? Not a surprise to you I am sure. They have a lot to pay attention to. Chapter 5321 Section 05 contains the obligations to be followed by tenants. A summary of some of those tenant obligations is below:

1. Keep the part of the premises they occupy safe and sanitary;

2. Dispose of all rubbish, garbage, and other waste in a clean, safe, and sanitary manner;

3. Keep the plumbing fixtures as clean as their condition permits;

4. Use and operate all electrical and plumbing fixtures properly;

5. Comply with all tenant requirements found in state and local housing, health, and safety codes;

6. Personally refrain and keep any other person who had permission to be on the premises from intentionally or negligently destroying, defacing, damaging, or removing any fixture, appliance, or other part of the premises;

7. Keep in good working order and condition any range, refrigerator, washer, dryer, dishwasher, or other appliances supplied by the landlord and required to be maintained by the tenant according to the terms and conditions found in a written rental agreement;

8. Conduct himself and require all other persons on the premises with consent of the tenant in a manner that will not disturb his neighbors' peaceful enjoyment of the premises;

9. Conduct himself and all other permitted guests on the premises in such a manner that they are not to violate any drug and substance abuse laws found in Chapters 2925 and 3719 of the Ohio Revised Code and municipal ordinances that are similar and relate to controlled substances;

10. The tenant cannot unreasonably withhold consent for the landlord to enter the dwelling to inspect the premises, make necessary repairs or other kinds of improvements, deliver parcels too large for the tenant's mail facility, supply necessary and agreed services, show the dwelling to prospective or actual purchasers, mortgagees, tenants, workmen, or contractors.

Depending upon which of the above circumstances apply, the landlord can recover any actual damages that result with reasonable attorney fees, terminate the rental agreement, and have the tenant evicted. There are also necessary procedures to invoke if the tenant, his children, or others allowed on the premises have committed a crime. Eviction can be required within 3 days according to Ohio law.

What Properties Are the Best to Own?

The simple answer is that it depends. And it depends on a lot of things. I did not have to struggle through all of those variables in order to ascend to the throne of a landlord king. My very astute father did that hard decision making for me for the most part. He had decades of "ruling" experience and I took my orders well, knowing I would one day need his imparted wisdom to rule the "Callahan Kingdom."

Based on my experiences and the wisdom passed on by my father, the best investment property is the 2 or 4 family-unit dwelling. First of all, you not only own the land and its value goes up over time, but you are also generating income from the rental leases and that provides money for you to live on. Of course, investing in a property with 30 units, for example, provides more income for the landlord, but the problems and tasks associated with an apartment complex that large multiply exponentially.

In later chapters of the book I will elaborate on some lessons I have learned about the best and worst kinds of properties to invest in, changes I would have made in investments if I had to do it over, and other lessons on being a landlord king that I have learned in my own experiences and from others.

Alas, we are now ready to get into real life experiences I have encountered along with lessons that I have learned from decades of "rule" trying to provide the best possible homes for many tenant citizens of Columbus. Naturally, a fair return on my investment was also a major motive in being a successful landlord. You will learn a lot from my experiences and stories about working with tenants, bailiffs, other law enforcement personnel, neighbors of my tenants, and others. You just may want to become a "landlord king." Let's move on to Chapter 4: The Nature and Types of Tenants and the perils associated with renting to the wrong tenants.

CHAPTER 4

SELECTING THE "RIGHT" TENANTS

Other than buying the best property possible for the dollars at your disposable selecting the right tenants is a very close second in terms of skill, insight, and predictability. Mistakes can and have been made. Not all who show up to rent are who they appear to be or say they are.

What is the Landlord King Looking for in a Prospective Tenant?

There is an easy answer, of course. You want someone that will pay the rent and do it on time, pay the utility bills, be a good neighbor, keep quiet, and keep the property and indoor and outdoor furnishings in top condition. Who is likely to do that? Experienced "landlord kings" know how to select those people but none score 100% in making those decisions I am sorry to say. Just think of some of the noisy and cranky neighbors who have had over the years whether or not you owned your home or rented. Duplexes and other multiunit residences have even more issues when it comes to your neighbor next door, across the back fence, or on the other side of the street.

Here are some of the key elements that go along way in helping me and other landlords in selecting the right tenants. Most will be no surprise.

1. They are employed and have some tenure in their employment. If they don't have a job or they are "job jumpers," it is a fairly easy prediction to make that they

are not going to pay the rent regularly and not on the date that it is due.

2. What is the prospective tenant's income? If, for example, 90 percent or more of their income is already obligated to other costs and loan payments, you might more than suspect that they are not going to be one of your most prompt tenants in paying the rent.

3. How long was the prospective tenant at their last residence? If they are "house jumpers," that portends late rent payments, damage to rental property, uncivil conduct as a tenant and neighbor, etc. There are reasons for moving and breaking a lease, for sure, such as changing jobs, but if moving continuously over short periods of time is part of their background, if indeed shows more than that.

4. Are they late for the scheduled appointment to view the property they want to rent? I have found this behavior to be predictive in identifying those who will not pay their rent on time either.

I need to rent to the best tenants I can identify from these items above and some standard qualifying elements that I have them submit on my rental application. After all, I cannot be with the tenants at all times (in fact, very little unless they are next door), so I need to select the best I can find. If lucky, I could chose the first shopper to look at the property or it may require visits and discussions with dozens before I am confident I have the right tenant.

** The overall best predictors for selecting the right tenants I have found are (1) their prompt payment of rent and (2) and their tenure in their last rental residence. It is fairly clear what these two elements predict for the landlord. They are likely to pay the rent on time and be good neighbors.

I will not rent to anybody who has been evicted in the last 7 years and the law in Ohio backs me up on this.

Standard Items on the Callahan Rental Application

By no means unique in all respects here are some items I have included on my rental application that needs to be filled out by the prospective tenant.

1. Basic identification information and the prospective tenant's reason for moving.

2. Their current landlord and the number of occupants who will be in the property they rent from me.

3. Previous addresses and how long they stayed there.

4. Employment information: employer; type of job; starting date; supervisor's name; and salary.

5. Rental history: have they ever broken a lease, been evicted, or filed for bankruptcy?

6. Bank account information: checking account; savings account, credit card, and bank.

7. Criminal history information: convictions for felony, sex crime, or crime of violence.

In addition, the prospective tenant must be 18 years of age and there is no upper age limit. I have had tenants in the 90's that were some of the best I have rented to.

Mistakes Can Be Made in Selecting the "Right Tenants"

Indeed the "right tenants" are not always selected. My father and I have made mistakes. While I allow no dogs or cats to reside at the rental property, who would believe that one of my tenants brought his own ALLIGATOR with him to be a permanent tenant and amble around. Needless to say that did not last long.

The future behavior of some people is hard to predict. There is a truism that most often works: *past performance is the best predictor of future behavior*. Those words of wisdom work in most venues: selecting the best students; picking the best college athletes for professional teams; selecting the right candidates for political office; eating at the right restaurants, choosing the best employees from a pool of applicants and on and on.

In Chapter 5 I will describe some of my experiences with some of the worst tenants I have chosen and had to contend with. Some stories are humorous; some are disheartening; some are nearly incredible.

CHAPTER 5

"OH, NO! THE WRONG TENANTS"

Wouldn't it be wonderful (oops, I almost said *awesome*) if every tenant you leased to was intelligent, civil, polite, caring, neighborly, and honorable as they used your buildings, appliances, furniture, and other possessions? You would indeed like to do business with them. Well, sorry, it "ain't" going to happen. No matter how diligent you are, sometimes you get the wrong tenants. It has happened to me and my father who once ruled the "kingdom" and passed it on to me.

In the brief stories below you will see some of the mistakes we made and perhaps be astounded at the actions of some of our tenants. Some of those tenant actions are bizarre enough to cause a landlord to lose sleep or even scream.

The first case described below was not on my property but on the property of one of my landlord colleagues.

1. The Alligator Keeper

I do not allow tenants to have pets on my properties, even those of the most common genre, dogs and cats. They often cause problems as you can imagine such as damage to the property, fear on the part of other tenants and neighbors, and nerve-wracking noise. This first case of getting the wrong tenant was not one that involved my property but the rental premises belonging to a landlord colleague.

Tenants were not supposed to have pets. This tenant did not have a dog or a cat. He had a 4-foot long alligator! It was kept outside in the summer but he took it inside during the winter. Very caring. The landlord told him that he must get rid of the alligator. The tenant saw nothing wrong with it. Finally a bailiff was called to the premises and told the tenant to get the alligator out of there. Even more surprising, the tenant called the police on the bailiff! He did not want anyone to "screw" with his alligator. In the end, the landlord won and the tenant moved on.

2. The Pole Dancers

Tenants are not supposed to alter or damage the premises. If it they have not read the lease even the most uninformed tenant should understand this kind of requirement. It is not their property. I headed for one of my rented dwellings to make a plumbing and/or electrical repair. I was shocked at my discovery after I entered the premises with my passkey. No one was home so I have this right to enter. Permission for entry in this kind of circumstance is covered in the lease.

Five young women were living at the dwelling. I rented to two young women. In the middle of the living room I discovered a dancer's pole. It turns out that the young women were running a business out of the living room and bedrooms. You guessed it. My tenants were entrepreneurs. They were running a brothel on my property. They always paid the rent on time. They had stayed two years before they were asked to leave.

3. The Artist Tenant, Etc.

I indeed appreciate those with artistic talent of any kind but where those exceptional people display their art can be a matter of concern. I rented to 3 men and it was not long after that 6 men occupied my premises. The unauthorized extras brought their own beds and other pieces of furniture. They put 3 extra beds in the basement. Yes, as you can imagine it was now a congested living quarter. There were even more tenants. He had 3 cats that he was not allowed to have according to a condition in the lease. But that was not the worst of it in my mind.

One or more of these tenants was an artist, a painter to be exact featuring abstract works, landscape, and portraits. To be even more specific we can call him an "interior decorator." Guess what surfaces he put his large paintings on. He painted more than four dozen pictures, which covered every wall and ceiling of the property that I leased to him. Can you imagine thinking that this action would be acceptable to the Landlord King, the owner of the property?

I took my own pictures of every location where he portrayed his artistic talent thinking that I might need this as evidence later on. The boys moved out, however, when I told them I had to sell the property.

4. The Hair Dyer

At another property I came to fix a problem with the toilet. Toilets are relatively easy to fix after you get a little experience with them. I knocked on the front door and got no answer. I went to the backdoor that lead into the kitchen and knocked and got no reply so I used my master key to open the kitchen door.

I surprised to find the woman tenant on the premises standing at the kitchen sink, bent over, and dying her hair. We both apologized and she said, "Go ahead and fix it." I wish she had answered the door. She was naked from the waist up and her breasts were clearly visible. She did not seem to be particularly bothered by my legitimate but surprise "intrusion." It took me about 10 minutes to repair the toilet and I was out of there.

5. The Furniture Mover

Most all of us can tell the difference between indoor and outdoor furniture. First of all they are made differently. This tenant was charged with improper storage on the exterior of the property.

I had provided the tenant with a stove, refrigerator, dishwasher, toilet, washer, and dryer. All else belongs to the tenant.

Here is the law, however. "Upholstered furniture, mattresses, materials and other similar products not designed, built, and manufactured for outdoor use unless such is in an enclosed porch or balcony violates Section 3332.289 Zoning Violation – Prohibited Uses and Activities. "

This tenant took indoor furniture from numerous locations inside the rental property and placed the items outside. Tenant said he did not know this was a violation of the zoning regulations. He was not evicted, but the indoor furniture was removed from the porch in compliance with the zoning code.

6. The Delinquent Renter

Would it surprise you that for one or numerous reasons some tenants don't pay their rent on time? I am sure it would not. The world runs a lot smoother for the tenant and the landlord if monthly rent payment is made on time.

One of my woman tenants paid her rent on time for about one year. Then, odd as it may sound, she stopped paying the rent. She as given notice to leave the premises and pay all unpaid water bills and a late fee of $50 and $25 per day until she returned the premises to the owner. The owner is me, of course.

A reason that she brought forward for not paying the rent was that she did not know who to give the payment to. That is odd since she had figured that out every month for a year and now she could not recall who to give the rent check to? She started paying the rent to my business, but eventually she moved out and on to wherever. Who knows what really caused her dilemma?

7. Two Busy Guys

Landlords who are doing their job sometimes show up at their rental properties at the strangest times. I think you will agree that this was one of those occasions. I was coming to the premises to make a repair and knocked on the door downstairs and I guess the tenants did not hear me. I moved to the second level of the building in order to knock on the door and gain entry or enter the property with my landlord passkey.

The door on the second level was one of those all glass doors that allowed a near complete view of the room's interior. I changed my mind about entering the room when I saw two men having sex in a bed inside the door. Ooops! Making the repair at a later time was a much better idea than doing the work immediately.

8. Disturbers of My Peace

I have always thought that an appreciation for peace and tranquility is an essential feature of the best tenants. That is even more important if the tenant is going to live next door to me. This is the account of two tenants who were my next-door neighbors.

They loved playing the radio extremely loud deep into the night and early morning. The walls vibrated because they played the music so loud. I told them they could not do that. Their answer was, "Yes we can. We can do whatever we want to do. We leased the place."

My answer was, "No you can't. I own the place." Things did not get any better and they stayed on the property for about a year and a half. Finally, they moved. Obviously there are limits on what a landlord can do in a circumstance like this one, but maybe the restrictions in matters like this are a little to confining for the landlord.

I could go on with story after story where tenants have exceed the limits of civility and common sense. Of course, most are good neighbors and make my job bearable and even enjoyable most of the time.

There are thousands of landlord/tenant stories that will amaze you and me. Take a look at this website below. It contains land/lord tenant stories, jokes, and excuses tenants make for not paying their rent. It also contains many helpful resources for landlords. The website is called The Landlord Protection Agency.

http://www.thelpa.com/lpa/excuses.html

Here are some excuses found on the website for not paying the rent:

Excuse of the Day for 5/6/14:
"I was going to pay on the 1st, but you upset me by sending me a reminder to pay. You don't need a reminder to pay your mortgage, do you?" No, that's whey I own and you rent. - G, Virginia

Excuse of the Day for 5/5/14:
"My dog and bird died the same week, I'm crushed." - Valhalla, LLC

Excuse of the Day for 4/27/14:
"I was on vacation (for 2 weeks) and no one had any money except me so I had to pay for everything!" Seriously? Well, I CANT afford to go on vacation seeing as I am paying for my rent and YOURS! - Kathy in Springfield Ma

Excuse of the Day for 4/6/14:
"My nephew stole the rent money from my wallet, here's the police report, I didn't press charges because he's a good boy." - Connie from Ohio

Let's move on to Chapter 6 and discuss some MAJOR TENANT PROBLEMS AND SOLUTIONS.

CHAPTER 6

MAJOR TENANT PROBLEMS AND SOLUTIONS

Problems abound in the rule of the landlord kingdom. You have already heard about many of those problems and what my remedies were. Those issues included tenants who don't pay rent, deface and destroy property, and cause disturbances in the neighborhood. This chapter will list and describe some of the most frequent and most perplexing problems.

This list of problems and their remedies can help you prepare for ruling your kingdom. I will also show you that you are not alone in maintaining order in the kingdom and success in your landlord king career. You have these allies: the courts; bailiffs; good lessees and neighbors; and, of course, the local police and sheriff departments.

Below are some of the major problems and solutions

1. Noisy Neighbors

They throw trash in your yard, entertain and house rowdy guests, play loud music continuously, and poke their nose into other peoples' business. But the loud music players are a far too frequent.

You can call the noisy neighbors (a good and bothered neighbor probably informed you) and tell them politely to shut down or turn off the loud music. They will often obey, but some start up the loud music again at a later hour.

You have an ally in getting them to "shut down" the music and "shut up." That ally is the local beat police officer. In my city of Columbus, Ohio loud noise and music cannot be played after 10 pm. You call the police, they will tell the disturbing tenant to shut the music down and if they do not and the police have to show up again, the tenants get cited for a violation of the city's ant-noise ordinance. One of these above remedies most always eliminates the problem. Those tenants who repeat the violation several times as you can imagine are prime candidates for eviction.

2. Tenants Who Fail To Pay The Rent

My tenants have to pay the rent by the third of every month. That is in the lease agreement. If they are late within reason they can pay the rent and a $50 late fee. If the persist in their delays to pay the rent, they are taken to court on an eviction request from me and about three weeks later they are indeed evicted. The court offers a very strong backing for the landlord in these cases. In a period in our history where many are choosing not to own a home, renters will be more prevalent and landlords will need the court even more. Business commentators say that many young couples do not want to be tied down to one job and have to sell a house if they take another job in another city and state. They change jobs more frequently now than they did in the past.

3. The "Overcrowded" House

Family and fellowship are wonderful support forces in all kinds of situations but they have limits when it comes to meeting the requirements of a tenant's lease. A landlord rents the property to a certain number of people. That means that others cannot move there and live for free or pay rent to the person who is the subject of the lease. I essentially lease to 1, 2, or 3 people at my properties. But you will probably not be surprised to find out that once the lease has started a tenant may move more people in. When this is discovered that also means that the person was dishonest in completing the lease document and signing it.

I would imagine now at this point in the book you know what the solution to this particular tenant problem is. The answer is eviction and there is little if any grounds for mercy. The tenants and the entire "crowd" are gone in a period of 3 weeks by order of the court. People who live next-door to these tenets who bring in an excess of roomers are dissatisfied when 5 additional people show up to live in a rental home that was made for 2 or 3. This overcrowding affects the quality of a neighborhood, for sure.

4. Pets

As you realize I do not allow my tenants to have pets. If they are caught with pets, they have 24 hours to rid the premises of the pets. If they do not, they are evicted. Over the course of my reign as landlord king I have had to deal with this pet issue many times. I suspect that people enter into the lease agreement realizing that want to violate it and bring in pets once they move in. Most of the time these are cats and dogs, but there are some other cases with my most weird case being the guy with the alligator. A dog may be man's best friend, but that friendship cannot be maintained on my rental properties.

It sounds cold, but it is necessary in order to maintain the property.

5. Unpaid Utility Bills

The tenants in my landlord kingdom must pay all utility bills to include water, heat, and electricity. To ensure that these bills are paid on time as required by the lease I have meters for all three services on the outside of the houses and apartments and I have employed a very reputable private company that reads all of the meters for me. That company is called Guardian, a good name for what they do. Guardian reads the meters once a month and if the utilities are not paid, the tenants are evicted.

6. The Running Toilet

Some problems for a landlord will simply not go away. One of the most persistent ones for me, and I suspect for other landlords, is the running toilet. We have all had this problem in our bathrooms at least once if not more in our lives. You probably know the most immediate solution that usually works the first time the problem occurs or during multiple times the problem surfaces.

Tenants call me and say the toilet is running and it will not stop and they are worried about their monthly water bill going up. That is a legitimate worry, but guess what? They can fix it on the spot. You can probably guess what I tell them: "Shake the handle a few times!" In most all cases the problem is solved. They are now "master plumbers" of sorts and can fix the problem when it occurs in the future. I don't hand out certificates for those who "pass the course" on how to fix the running toilet but perhaps I should.

7. The Light Went Out

Tenants living in the kingdom sometimes have a light go out and they call me for the solution to fix it. Can you guess my answer on this one? I bet you can. "Put in a new light bulb!" It is that simple, but they call me on this one and I have to respond as a caring landlord king with politeness and care. I do not want them "living in the dark."

8. The Trash Man Didn't Pickup My Waste

There are some very rare occasions where a trash man will miss some waste cans or trash bags, but it is indeed rare. What a job to have, collecting trash. I have never cared to do that for a living.

Nevertheless, tenants will call and say the trash man missed their waste loads even when then set it outside. There are some fundamentals about getting your trash collected such as is it all in the waste can or a bag, and there is that very big one: "It has to be next to the curb!" Duh! Some are not careful about that and they call me when the trash man "missed" their collection this week. On one such case that I followed up on I went to the residence and found that the tenant put the trash out right next to their front porch and I suppose that they thought the trash collector was going to go up the walk to the porch and get their trash. He did not do that and should not be expected to do so.

I "schooled" the tenant about having to place the trash on the curb in a timely manner and that was the end of the problem for this tenant.

9. The Kitchen Sink Drain Is Plugged Up

I have had to entertain so many of these complaints about the kitchen sink drain being plugged up that I took an action on my part that essentially eliminated this problem. I used to provide a garbage disposal unit in the kitchen sinks of my tenants. I do not do that anymore.

I would get call after call from tenants saying the kitchen sink drain was plugged up, and these drains almost always were connected with a garbage disposal unit. Here is what happens. The garbage disposal is supposed to be used only with cold water to prevent the expanding of some foods in the drain and to keep it from sticking to the pipes. Both instructions for the garbage disposal unit and landlords pass on this information to tenants usually. After a plethora of calls about this never-ending problem, I have stopped providing a garbage disposal unit.

Can you guess what the biggest food product "enemy' of the drain is? The answer is lettuce. It just won't "die." It plugs up drains almost without ceasing and some tenants have the idea that it dissolves in water. It does not.

10. Leasing To Students

I do not lease to college students for a number of reasons. The first reason is that they often only want to lease for 9 months and not a year or more. Secondly, they often do not care for the premises very well since they are going to school, studying, having parties, and who knows what else.

I have and will lease to the parents of students but that lease must be for one year. Even a little oversight of the students on the part of the parents can help improve their tenant etiquette and assist in taking good care of the landlord's property.

11. Leasing To Section 8 Housing Tenants

Many worthy and needy tenants are assisted by Section 8 Housing subsidies. Let it be known that many tenants using Section 8 subsidies are not good tenants and do not take care of the property very well, have disturbances on the property, and do not pay their very small portion of the rent. Under Section 8, the client pays $25 a month out of their pocket and the government pays the rest. Thanks for paying your taxes. You are legitimately helping many but also caring for a small portion of renters who are abusing the system in a number of ways.

The good news for the landlord kings is that they do not have to rent or lease to Section 8 qualified tenants and there is no penalty in not doing so. I do not do it. I have enough problems and issues to manage now without adding more that would accompany renting to Section 8 tenants.

You have just read a list of the major tenant problems and my suggestions for managing and eliminating them. By this point in the book, you can see that you can make a lot money being a landlord king and leasing property, but it is not easy as many who have tried it for a period of time soon come to realize. The exit "their kingdom" and try a different path to wealth, health, and happiness. I stuck it out and I trust the information I have provided in the book thus far will assist you. We need great landlord kings. That is without question.

In Chapter 7 below, "It Is Time To Leave: The Problems and Perils of Eviction" we will examine this troubling but necessary process of eviction.

CHAPTER 7

"IT'S TIME TO LEAVE:" THE PROBLEMS AND PERILS OF EVICTION

Can you imagine what it is like to be "thrown out" of your home? Of course, in most all cases the tenants under lease are not literally "thrown out" but they are forced to leave under order from the court based on the lease violations presented to the court during the eviction process. The overwhelming majority of eviction cases are a result of the tenant not paying the rent. That has been my experience.

In total, I have been involved in about four-dozen evictions. The eviction cases that my father and I initiated were all the result of tenants not paying the rent. The lease that the tenants sign requires that they pay the rent by the 5th of each month. They can stay in the premises if they are late up to a total of 3 days, but they must pay a $50 late fee. If they have not paid the rent by the end of the 3-day grace period, eviction is the only solution.

The Eviction Attorney

To start the eviction process I call my eviction attorney, a major ally in the "rule of the landlord kingdom." I write out a copy of the 3-day notice to leave and I post it on the outside of the main door of the residence of the erring tenant. The tenant has 3 days to leave. If the tenant is not out in 3 days, I send a copy of the 3-day notice and the lease to my attorney.

My attorney files the paperwork in court. The court hears the case within 3 weeks. If I win in court I have my attorney file a writ of restitution. This writ of restitution gives the bailiff the right to "red tag" the door of the residence. The "red tag" document orders the erring tenant to move out immediately. If I get the key back from the bailiff that means the tenant moved out as ordered.

If the tenant to be evicted does not move out, I call the bailiff and meet with him at the property to do a "set out" of the delinquent tenant's belongings. The tenant gets no more extra time to vacate the premises. The "set out" means that all of the tenant's belongings (furniture, personal items, etc.) are set outside in front of the property between the curb and the sidewalk. This is done within 1 hour. I change the locks on the doors while the delinquent tenant is moving out. If the tenants have been late paying the rent before, they are probably not surprised that they are now being evicted. Most of the tenants who get evicted have a "now you got me attitude" and cause no trouble at this point in the process.

I have used the same attorney in all of the cases of eviction concerning my properties. The process costs me some money, however. That cost is $350.

The Court Magistrate

A magistrate in the local court actually makes the eviction. A magistrate is a lower level judge in the municipal court system of my city, Columbus, Ohio.

The order to vacate the premises now has the full force of the law when the eviction notice has been taped to the outside of the tenant's front door. All in all in takes about 21 days for the eviction process to transpire. It works for all landlords and has worked for me, as I mentioned above, about four-dozen times.

Court Bailiff

Another critical ally in the eviction process is the court bailiff. It is this officer that makes sure the tenant is out on time. Being at the scene to make sure this happens could be a tense situation, but I have had no serious problems concerning my rental properties.

The bailiffs can be armed and sometimes are. They also have a radio that connects them with the police department in case they would need assistance.

The Best Solution to Avoid the Eviction Process

I bet you can guess what is the best predictor of whether or not a new tenant is going to promptly pay their rent. Yes, the key element in figuring that out is whether or not they have paid their rent in the past at other rented properties. I usually know how many times a tenant applicant has been evicted previously for not paying the rent on time and I simply do not rent to the chronic violators. One of the applicants to lease a residence of mine asked if his 6 previous evictions were too many and would it prohibit him from getting a lease with me. I answered, "No" to his request to lease.

One of my tenants was in bed when his eviction was to take place. He asked a silly question, "Am I moving today?" I said, "Yes." He then asked me if he could take a shower before he was evicted. My answer was, "No."

I have one other indicator that I use concerning the likelihood that a tenant would pay the rent on time and comply with other tenant requirements. Do they show up on time to view the residence they want to lease? If they are more than 10 minutes late, I do not grant them the right to lease my property.

Another Crazy Eviction Story

Here is another eviction story from the plethora of crazy stories about the process that can be found on the Internet. This one is from Joe and posted on memebee.com

"When I was livin' in the States, I heard about these dudes who got evicted from their apartment for using it as a motorcycle repair shop. By the time they were discovered, the apartment was an absolute mess. Grease everywhere, filth smeared all over the walls with palm prints, the drapes were destroyed from havin' 'em used to wipe off the oil and grease on the scooters they were fixin'. "

...So they got the boot.

I take great pride in providing and maintaining comfortable living quarters for tenants and their families in the larger properties. But I cannot do that if the rent money is not being paid at the appropriate time. I have investments to make in order to maintain and improve the rental property and that takes money. Moreover this is how I make my living so I need a paycheck too and those dollars come from the tenants. Over the course of my time in the landlord business, most all of the tenants have been dutiful in paying their rent on time. I have been blessed, for sure.

CHAPTER 8

CONCLUSIONS, REFLECTIONS, AND ADVICE

As of this writing I am close to leaving the "throne" of the landlord king. I have mixed feelings about this life change, for sure. After spending a near half-century in the business of providing satisfying living quarters for tenants, resolving their rental problems (even sometimes when the problems are not real), and reaping the financial benefits of owning more than 4 dozen residences I have clearly decided it is time to leave.

Objectives for Chapter 8

You have read the previous 7 chapters of the book and have gotten more than a glimpse of what it is like to devote your life to being a landlord king. The profession is challenging, more than occasionally frustrating, and open to all who would choose to do it them selves. I want to do several things in this last chapter that may be helpful to you in terms of just knowing more about the profession and/or assist you in deciding if you want to become a part of the royalty in a long line of landlord rulers.

1. Summarize some key points about being a successful landlord;

2. Identify some of the joys of the profession;

3. Provide some advice for new and prospective landlords;

4. Identify some personal traits needed in the profession;

5. Mention a few of my most memorable moments;

6. Name some things I will miss about being a landlord and some things I will not miss.

Key Points about the Landlord Profession

I will mention first that the landlord profession is hard work! I cannot hide that. This is probably not news to you after reading the previous 7 chapters. To get to the point of success where you have the rent rolling in on time each month from reliable tenants living in safe and comfortable living conditions takes major effort on the landlord's part. You are the "dad" or "mom" for the tenant family. When things go wrong, you are often the one to fix it or arrange having the problem fixed. If you are moving into the landlord business from a job where you worked 8-10 hours a day and off on the weekends, do not expect that when you become a landlord king.

As your number of properties increase, the problems and complaints increase exponentially. But your insights and skills in fixing these problems increase also if you have added properties one or a few at a time. You will feel good about knowing what to do with some of the recurring problems across your "kingdom." You will have assistance such as some of those allies I mentioned in a previous chapter (magistrate, bailiff, etc.) but you will also contract with various other full or part time employees that you have hired to do repair work of one kind of another, so you are not alone. I have employed more than 60 workers in various capacities in my career who fix all sorts of things when repairs or modifications are needed at a residence. Allow me to mention it again, being a landlord is hard work.

Joys in Being a Landlord

It will not be news that I am in the business for profit. Getting the rent checks in on time makes the life of the landlord king worth living. Your investment in properties will grow and you will take great pride in seeing your bank account increase regularly. This means you have made good decisions to get you to this point and you will continue to make them as your investments grow. The best predictor of future performance is past behavior. Every psychologist and anyone with common sense know that.

I am also very pleased when the tenants are satisfied with the living quarters I have provided for them and they work hard to maintain the property in good condition. I enjoy their gratitude and am pleased to realize they will be occupying my property with only the minimal assistance expected from a landlord.

I should also mention that being a landlord in and of itself is a matter of distinction. Relatively few people work in such a capacity so I am sure and have told them that I have a career that most people would never consider entering because of the hard work and business acumen needed to be successful as a landlord. Many people who start out as a landlord leave after a short period of time since they lack the needed knowledge and skills. I am proud to be a landlord.

Personal Traits Needed to Be a Landlord

Let's start with intelligence. When your kingdom includes dozens or more families landlords not so bright are not going to be able to identify and manage all of the things that need to be done. As I have said, intelligence is at the top of the list in predicting how well someone will do in just about any job. Doing a thorough analysis of the applicants for a residence and selecting the one that is going to pay the rent on time and keep the property in good condition is at the top of the list requiring intelligence. The best landlord kings are great social engineers whether they know that field of study or not. They are living it and need to know how to read their tenant applicants and current tenants.

The landlord must also be disciplined and orderly in the performance of the key tasks required. They are not running a military unit but they have to know what to do and when. Overlooking key tasks, such as being sure the appliances are working properly at the residences, and seeing that things are done in a timely fashion can please the tenants, maintain the property value, and avoid tragedies. A fire or flood in the house might be good examples of bad things that can happen.

Patience with your fellow man is a virtue that seems to be less and less prevalent in the 21st century. Why I am not sure, but exercising patience in your approach to all problems allows for better analysis of a problem and then deciding what to do about it. You have probably heard that one of the first things that should be done about some problems is do nothing. Some things fix themselves. This is not an option in an emergency, of course, but waiting awhile to see what will happen with some existing problems is often the wise thing to do. In dealing with tenants, some times they figure out what to do about a minor problem on their own.

Advice for New and Prospective Landlords

Here is a major point of advice. Never take a personal check from a new tenant and then give them the keys to the residence. That check may not be backed up with money in the bank. When a tenant establishes a record of honesty and diligence in paying the rent personal checks are likely to be valid.

In addition, never rent to a tenant who has been evicted one or more times. This one is simple since the same thing is likely to happen again. Evictions and setouts are not fun for anybody.

If a tenant applicant does not show up in time to view the residence they want to rent, it may be wise to rent to another applicant. I have found that being prompt for the viewing of the residence is a good indicator of whether or not they tenant applicant will pay the rent on time.

What I Will Not Miss about Being a Landlord

I will not miss getting calls from tenants on the weekends, especially when they involve matters that can wait or the problems that can be fixed by the tenant who has common sense. Tenants need common sense to make the landlord's life a little easier.

I indeed will not miss going to eviction court and then having to be present at the set out with the court bailiff. This takes time and is an uncomfortable experience for all.

You may find this one a but unbelievable, but I will not miss answering phone calls from prospective tenants who ask how many bedrooms a property has when the sign out in front of the residence for lease says how many bedrooms there are inside the property.

My advice to new tenants concerning phone calls on the weekend is this: "Do not call me on the weekends unless the house is on fire (call the fire department) by calling 911 or if you are hungry, call a donut service or pizza parlor that delivers food. Many do. I have had as many as 100 phone calls on a weekend.

Conclusion

What will I miss about being a landlord king? Most of all I will miss seeing my sister, Carol Pozz, on Mondays when we go over all of the bills before she writes every one of the checks. Many thanks to Carol Pozz for taking care of all of the books. I could not have done this job with out her dedication and work.

I guess I might miss such events as the woman I mentioned earlier who was half naked washing her hair in the sink when I showed up at the property and she was not bothered by my presence! It happened as I mentioned earlier, but I am kidding about missing such an event.

Let me be honest with you, when I have sold all of my properties and the kingdom has been passed on to others, I will not miss any of the duties and experiences involved in being a successful landlord. I will not know the whole truth about that until all of my 54 units in 26 houses have been sold and I am out of the business. Then I may see more of what I miss. But as for now, I am looking forward to living that American dream, the life of leisure most find in retirement.

Those of you who will choose to be a landlord or who currently are, may I wish you the very best! Have fun. Life is short.